How to Write

HOW TO WRITE

derek beaulieu

Talonbooks

Talonbooks
Box 2076, Vancouver, British Columbia, Canada V6B 3S3
www.talonbooks.com

Typeset in Adobe Garamond and printed and bound in Canada.
Printed on 100% post-consumer recycled paper.

First Printing: 2010

The publisher gratefully acknowledges the financial support of the Canada
Council for the Arts; the Government of Canada through the Book Publishing Industry Development Program; and the Province of British Columbia
through the British Columbia Arts Council and the Book Publishing Tax
Credit for our publishing activities.

Library and Archives Canada Cataloguing in Publication

Beaulieu, D. A. (Derek Alexander), 1973–
How to write / Derek Beaulieu.

ISBN 978-0-88922-629-6

I. Title.

PS8553.E223H69 2010   C818'.54   C2009-906971-7

For Madeleine

Contents

Nothing Odd Can Last   11
And Then There Were None   15
The Editor: A Detective Story   19
Wild Rose Country   21
Cross It over It   23
I Don't Read   25
I Can See the Whole Room … and There's Nobody in It!   27
If You Have It   35
A Chain Saw   37
How to Edit: A   39
How to Write   45

Notes   67
Acknowledgements   71

Shall we for ever make new books, as apothecaries make new mixtures, by pouring only out of one vessel into another? Are we for ever to be twisting, and untwisting the same rope?
—*Laurence Sterne*

But when shall we actually write books like catalogues?
—*Walter Benjamin*

Nothing Odd Can Last

Are the bawdy passages and double entendres important in this book?

Could it have been omitted?

Does the author guide his pen or does his pen guide him?

Does she have redeeming qualities?

Does the novel demonstrate that there can be postmodern texts before post-modernism?

Do you think the author intended to end the novel with the ninth volume?

How do we account for the author's strikingly unsentimental treatment, at times, of such topics as love and death?

How does the seventh volume, in which the narrator describes his travels through Europe, relate to the rest of the book?

How ironical is their presentation?

How much control do you think the writer has over the mixture of digression—both kinds mentioned above—and the narrator's history?

How sentimental and gushy is the writer of this book?

If the latter is true, what justification can there be for that?

If you were a reader like the Lady, who reads "straight forwards, more in quest of the adventures, than of the deep erudition and knowledge," how would you feel about the novel?

In what way are such details important to the author's method?

In what way is it possible to reconcile the statement that the book will "be kept a-going" for forty years with the contention that the novel is completed?

Is it legitimate for an author to require—or even request—that the reader do things like "imagine to yourself," replace misplaced chapters, and put up with omitted chapters?

Is kindheartedness necessarily mawkishness?

Is she as stupid as she seems?

Is the author in control of his digressions (and merely affecting their spontaneity), or does the story actually run away from him and have to be reined back in?

Is the writer unable to present a straightforward story, or does he deliberately frustrate the reader?

Is there any importance to this, or is it just the author's bawdiness?

Is there sufficient justification for such passages in the book?

Or should the reader say to heck with it?

What are some of the qualities that the writer of the book has inherited from his forebears?

What does this indicate about the writer's plan and his control of what he was doing?

What evidence is there that the narrator's childhood traumas actually influence his adult personality?

What is the author's attitude toward science?

What is the effect of the precise visual details given in the book?

What is the effect of the narrator's frequent addresses to his audience?

What is the relationship between the "I" who narrates the story and the author?

What kinds of scenes receive this treatment?

Which predominates?

Why or why not?

Would it make sense to interpret the novel psychoanalytically?

Would you argue for or against his statement?

Would you rather that they were deleted from it?

And Then There Were None

One two three four five six seven eight nine and ten.
                          —*Gertrude Stein*

One two three four!   —*The Ramones*

1.
another two all some all some seven eight one one five a swarm
     five one a hundred a hundred a hundred one hundred sixty-
     five every half some two one or two thirty thousands a
     couple some half ten fifteen eighty another hundred a bit a
     few several six only one the lot one eight

2.
a little group four two one five one three one a lot a lot three a
     mere cluster two three one two double the number one a
     queer lot this lot one a queer one one one hundreds and
     hundreds 8 another one two eight ten one ten one nine nine
     one eight eight one seven seven one six six one five five one
     four four one four four one three three one two two one one
     one none one or two all two three very few one two

3.

a little group some many ten ten ten two one twenty nine twenty-
one nothing ten one once one two or three one two two two
one two another each one two or three

4.

all two one one ought a couple another one two one one ought

5.

one twelve one two ten lots twenty-eight twenty-nine another
some more three or four fifteen sixteen three three three

6.

some few nine two one one some ten one seven eight eight ten ten
two two ten ten ten nine eight eight eight

7.

two one twenty once two one two twelve two two ten eight ten
one nine nine one eight two one one three

8.

one one one one two one three three one one the other two three
one two two two five the only one two three one two two
five three eight

9.

two two a hundred hundred three two one five seven two seven
one one one one one ten seven seven one one one none one
two three one one one several one one or more one or more
one none no one once two a few two two one two eight three
one seven one all each and every one

10.

one one one three one two one or more five two one two one one
twenty-four twenty three none one one two one nine two
two two two four four four four four seven one one

11.

eight nine twenty-five twenty-five ten six seven six three-quarters
both half a couple one none six six six six

12.

half one one five eleven one one four one five four five one four
three four one five one two three one one

13.

One one one three five five five five one four five two a quarter
three twenty four twenty four a quarter four five five three
four five a quarter six twenty six four one four one half half
one three two five four one one

14.

four two four one four one four one two one one one six ten four
a thousand fourteen one two three one half half one two two
one one two one three

15.

three twenty-four one three one one one two one twenty four one
three one one two one both one one one one one two one two

16.

a thousand two one one two one two nine one one three two one
one none

Epilogue.

Ten two three one a lot nine ten two two one one ten ten ten one
ten one two thirty-six eight ten two 11 three one three one
one hundred one two one one ten two two one twenty-one
one two one one seven one a quarter two one two one one
three one one three one one ten four four one ten

The Editor: A Detective Story

A city editor, at lunch with a colleague, pulled at his cigarette and talked.

"Oh, for—lay off it, will you?" said the city editor peevishly.

The editor spread out his hands. The editor frowned. The editor was emphatic. The editor laughed grimly.

The editor smiled. His companion rose as well, but it was evident that the editor's theory had taken firm hold on his mind. The editor paused in the doorway.

"Well," said the editor, "you won't let it go any further?"

Tall, reticently good-looking and well, if inconspicuously, clothed and groomed, he by no means seemed the typical detective that the editor had spoken of so scornfully.

Cal-Alta 1978 Chevron Supreme Motor Oil Huile moteur SAE 5W-30 API SM 946mL 1 Quart Formulated with Formulée avec ISO SYN Technology / Technologie Homolougée pour American Petroleum Institute for Gasoline Engines Certified Moteurs à essence Water 737 737 End play ground zone 405 Hillhurst Teleride 974-4000 + stop number 8043 WYD-867 expiry date 03/31/2006 Hyundai Elantra Alberta June Alberta WYD-867 Alberta 08 080142376 Wild Rose Country Alberta 07 07041159211 Water 733 Nissan X-Trail Stadium SE "A Good Deal Better" Alberta May Alberta EZX-720 Alberta 09 0901445172 Alberta 08 0804563930 Stadium 729 Mazda 3 Ontario 09 Jan ACZP964 Yours to Discover Country Hills Toyota Yaris Alberta Nov Country Hills Blvd. At Deerfoot Tr. 290-1111 Alberta ETZ-638 Alberta 08 Toyota Country Hills Alberta 07 Toyota 727 Dueck GM on marine Mar Alberta Alberta DPZ-885 Alberta 08 Wild Rose Country Alberta 09 touring sedan Buick Buick Riviera Alberta May Alberta JHE-409 Alberta 08 Wild Rose Country Alberta 09 R Riviera Managed by Emerald Management & Realty Ltd. 237-8600 Sorry no vacancy for other locations please call 237-8600 Lumina Alberta Sep Alberta KRY-821 08 Wild Rose Country 721 No Soliciting Please keep off lawn until dry Green Drop Child Security lock when engaged door opens only from outside Printed in U.S.A. Pt. No. 10154456 24 hour roadside assistance 1-800-268-6800 Assistance Routière 24 heures Alberta Mar Alberta ELN-155

Alberta 08 Wild Rose Country Alberta 09 Jetta Varisty Chrysler Dodge Jeep Calgary Alberta Pacifica Chrysler Dodge Jeep Alberta JCW-655 Alberta 08 Varsity 07 Chrysler Ellsworth GAg GAg Expires last day of Apr Alberta H Civic VRU-845 Alberta 08 Wild Rose Country 07 CX Ridley's Maxxis Ellsworth Marzucchi cannondale Fresh Toyota Echo Precision Toyota Brandon Manitoba Alberta Jan Alberta EKW-264 Alberta 08 Wild Rose Country Alberta 09 715 Alberta Jun Alberta BTE-274 Accord Alberta 08 Crowfoot Village Honda 07 Crowfoot Village Honda V6 Discover Real Estate Ltd. SOLD C/S Cathrine Watson 510-7142 233-0706 350Z Nissan Alberta Apr Alberta FGE-120 Alberta 08 Wild Rose Country Alberta 09 Z Windstar Metro Ford Ford Alberta Oct Alberta KWY-173 Wild Rose Country Alberta 08 LX Traction Control Auto security warning vehicle secured Plymouth Alberta May Alberta CEA-384 Alberta 09 Wild Rose Country Alberta 08 Voyager LE Private Property Unauthorized vehicles will be ticketed and towed at owner's expense Infiniti G35 Alberta Sep Alberta NCU-058 Wild Rose Country Alberta 09 Charlesglen Toyota Corolla S Crowfoot Village Automall 241-0888 Alberta Jun Alberta MHU-306 Alberta 09 Charlesglen Toyota Northland Pontiac Buick GMC Grand Am GT Pontiac Alberta May Alberta YEP-658 Northland Alberta 09 Villager LS www.albertabeef.org Alberta Mar Alberta DCA-405 Alberta 08 Wild Rose Country Alberta 09 709 Cal-Alta 1978

CROSS IT OVER IT

Cross it over it, bring it up through it, then back down; pull it underneath it and to the right, back through it and to the right again so that it is inside out; bring it across the front from right to left; pull it up through it again; bring it down through it in front; using both hands, tighten carefully and draw it up.

Cross it over it; bring it around and behind it; bring it up; pull it through it; bring it around front, over it from right to left; again, bring it up and through it; bring it down through it in front; using both hands, tighten it carefully and draw it up.

Cross it over it; turn it back underneath it; continue by bringing it back over in front of it again; pull it up and through it; hold the front of it loosely with your index finger and bring it down through it; remove your finger and tighten it carefully by holding it and sliding it up.

Start with it under it; take it over and under it; pull it down and tighten; take it over to the right; pull it up, behind it; bring it through it and tighten it gently.

I Don't Read

If a tutorial doesn't have code I don't read it. Ten Reasons Why I Don't Read Your Blog. Sorry David I don't read anything apart from stories. "I don't read blogs, but I DO read …" I don't read newspapers or magazines anymore, at least not printed versions. "I don't read Slate!" he snapped. "Why would I read that?" I don't read books. Five reasons why I don't read mail on the Nokia 770. He says, "I suppose it would be interesting, but I don't read reviews. I don't want to believe the bad stuff and I don't want to believe the good stuff." I don't read criticism. "I suppose it would be interesting, but I don't read reviews." I don't read my blog either. "I don't read that much sports journalism." I don't encourage this; even with friends, I don't read things that aren't finished. However, strictly as a matter of prudence, it's best that I don't read your work. I don't read anymore, but I'd like to know what Steve Jobs has to say. I don't read DAT files, Database and Reporting. I don't read enough. Why I Don't Read Mysteries Anymore. I don't read Nigerian Newspapers. Why I don't read Fox News. Wow! Thanks for that! You've made me feel a bit better about the fact that I don't read my Bible every day either. I don't read them—I don't have time; I scan them. The title explains it all: I don't read. I like his blog, I like him, I value what he has to say, however for one reason or another I don't read his blog that often. Sounds like … I don't read INTO what is said. I don't read that language, but there are some useful links from that. I don't read books, I read e-books, Seriously though, I don't read books, my reading skills are reserved. But I don't read text printed in Braille font. I don't read yellow journals, not even as I wait in the checkout line. I don't read the sports section. Another reason I don't read them is that I've got a great network of filters. Why I don't read 8-Bit Theater. Oh no, I don't read the blogs—you couldn't pay me to read the blogs. I don't read any women bloggers. Because I don't read these books, I can't comment on the review. Hey, I don't read Arabic. As a result, I don't read their work as often. If you ain't a feed, I don't read … I don't read German. I don't read books about surfers and other unrelated factoids. That said, I don't read so much for fun on the side, because I am already reading so much I hardly have time and I enjoy what I do. Why I Don't Read the Newspaper. I Don't Read Nearly Enough These Days. I don't read Maureen Dowd. Buy this—I don't read your blog either. Agreed, I don't read newspapers too often (prefer my Google reader—and no English one here for that matter …) for the news, but as for books? If I don't read it, no one else will. That's okay, I don't read. I suspect we were all exaggerating a bit. I don't read MegaTokyo. I don't read any sports any more, save for an occasional visit to MLB.Com. I track around 700 blogs—however I don't read them all (I scan) and I wouldn't do that on a daily basis. 40 Responses to "Why I don't read theology blogs." I don't read books. 5 Reasons I Don't Read Your Blog and How to Change That. If I don't read regularly, I feel stressed. Warning messages, but I don't read Russian. "I don't read newspapers or magazines anymore either." Just because I don't read the dead trees doesn't mean other people don't. Maybe I don't read good but where does it say anything about reading skills? You might as well say "I don't read books" or "my brain is full." If I don't read it my soul be lost, nobody's fault but mine / Ah, Lord, Lord, nobody's fault but mine / If I don't read it my soul be lost. I don't read BOOKS I read POETRY. I don't read unless it is on a computer. I don't read stuff.

I Can See the Whole Room … and There's Nobody in It!

My work is right where it is […] definitely not a window into the world.

—*Roy Lichtenstein*

1

Look Mickey, I've hooked a big one!!

Tweet

It's … It's not an **engagement ring**. Is it?

I can see the whole room … **and there's nobody in it**!

I am supposed to report to a Mr. Bellamy. I wonder what he's like.

Knock Knock

2

-R-R-R-R-Ring!!

Viip!

Ziing

I tried to reason it out! I tried to see things from Mom and Dad's viewpoint! I tried not to think of Eddie, so my mind would be clear and common sense could take over! But Eddie kept coming back …

I have something for you to eat in the kitchen, dear …

I'm not hungry mother! **Please**, I just want to go to my room! Forget it! Forget me! I'm fed up with your kind!

Why, Brad darling, this painting is a **masterpiece**! My, soon, you'll have all of **New York** clamoring for your work!

Arrrrff!

Flatten—Sand fleas!

THUNG!

The exhausted soldiers, sleep-less for five and six days at a time, always hungry for decent chow, suffering from the tropical fungus infections, kept fighting!

TAKKA TAKKA

As I started clipping a **MIG's** tail …

This hot-shot jet outfit I'm in will treat me like a vet pilot when I return from my **No.1** wingding with a report of—target destroyed!

BRATATAT!

That was their mistake—because it gave me more targets than I could shoot at …

No. 4! One more to make **Ace**!

BRATTATA

Tex!

BLAM

Take Cover!

Live Ammo

Right now—if they're watchin' me—they've got to make up their minds whether I **don't** know they're here—and will pass by—lettin' the outfit be sucked into a trap—or whether I **know** they're here—and am about to fire at them but where did they come from? Not the sea—we've had our eyes glued to it! And we know there ain't an air field on this island! Where'd they come from? **Where'd they come from!**

Just then …

BLANG

TZING!

BWEEE!

Ha! Ha! Ha!

I … I'll think about it

3

CRAK!

Now mes petits ... pour **la France**!

Betty! Betty! Betty! Betty!

I know how you must feel, Brad ...

Although he holds his brush and palette in his hands, I know his heart is always with me!

That's the way—it **should** have **begun**! But it's hopeless!

Hello ...

I don't care! I'd rather sink—than call Brad for help!

It is ... with me!

I pressed the fire control ... and ahead of me rockets blazed through the sky ...

WHAAM!

Torpedo ... **LOS**!

Okay, Hot-Shot, Okay! I'm pouring!

VOOMP!

What? Why did you ask **that**? What do you know about my **image duplicator**?

As soon as I throw this switch, those light-impulses—in Khandara—on the island of Rhodes—and near the museum—hidden by my mirage duplicates before they tried to steal those souvenirs—will go into operation!

VAROOM!

I think Von Karp should enjoy this little game!

4

Oh, Jeff … I love you too … but …

Sweet Dreams Baby!

WHAM

Good morning … Darling!

Ohhh … alright …

No thank you!

We rose up slowly … as if we didn't belong to the outside world any longer … like swimmers in a shadowy dream … who didn't need to breathe …

As I opened fire, I knew why Tex hadn't buzzed me … if he had … BRAT!

Vicki! I—I thought I heard your voice!

Reckon **not**, sir! This has become sort of a **personal** matter!

Help!!

5

This must be the **place**!

M-maybe he became ill and couldn't leave the studio!

Grrrrrrrrr!

Sweet Dreams Baby!

POW!

The melody haunts my reverie …

6

Whaam!
Nok! Nok!
Pop!

7

See that baldheaded **guy** over there? That's "Curly" **Grogan**! He and his mob **run** half the rackets in this town!

Look Mickey, I've hooked a **big** one!!

If You Have It

If you have it you don't need it. If you need it you don't have it. If you have it you need more of it. If you have more of it you don't need less of it. You need it to get it, and you certainly need it to get more of it. But if you don't already have any of it to begin with, you can't get any of it to get started which means you really have no idea how to get it in the first place, do you? You can share it, sure. You can even stockpile it if you'd like but you can't fake it. Wanting it. Needing it. Wishing for it. The point is if you've never had any of it, ever, people just seem to know.

A Chain Saw

A chain saw is wisely resplendent. Any cab driver can write a love letter to the paycheck around the inferiority complex, but it takes a real warranty to seek some chain saw.

Indeed, the gentle tomato barely assimilates a blood clot from the stovepipe.

Furthermore, the sheriff gets stinking drunk and a corporation behind the warranty goes deep sea fishing with an orbiting power drill.

Now and then, the satellite recognizes the microscope.

How to Edit: A

It was his intention to edit them with the necessary notes and vocabularies; but, so far as I know, the only specimens which appeared in print were those he laid before the *American Philological Association*, in 1872.

Should this attempt meet with favour, I propose to edit after the same plan some others of the less known and less edited portions of Cicero's writings.

I had imagined every other sort of strange and sudden preferment, of frantic proprietors asking me at a moment's notice to edit their papers, or of taking up some great and responsible position, but never of carrying by assault 1 Wellington Street.

You won't have anything to do but ask people to write novels and edit them.

In 1869 he went north to edit the *Edinburgh Daily Review*, and made a mess of it; in 1870 he represented that journal as field-correspondent in the Franco-Prussian War, was present at Sedan, and claimed to have been the first Englishman to enter Metz.

It may seem peculiar to any but an inhabitant of this renowned city of Caneville, that one of *our* nation should venture on the task of bringing to the notice of the world the memoir I have undertaken to edit.

I begin almost to despair of ever seeing more of the Mabinogeon; and yet if some competent Welshman could be found to edit it carefully, with as literal a version as possible, I am sure it might be made worth his while by a subscription, printing a small edition at a high price, perhaps two hundred at five guineas.

In later years, after Amorbach's death, the marked advance in the output of the firm as regards type and paper and title-pages and designs may be attributed to Froben, who was man of business enough to realize the importance of getting good men to serve him—Erasmus to edit books, Gerbell and Oecolampadius to correct the proofs, Graf and Holbein to provide the ornaments. A measure of the confidence which Erasmus subsequently reposed in both his judgment and his good faith is that in 1519 and 1521, when he had decided to publish some more of his letters, he just sent to Beatus bundles of the rough drafts he had preserved, and told him to select and edit them at his discretion.

The rhapsody of gratitude was never sent, and for a peculiar reason: just about the time of writing I came to an arrangement with Smith & Elder to edit their new magazine, and to have a contribution from T. was the publisher's and editor's highest ambition.

"You can't do it," she concluded, "unless you are prepared to keep half the world's literature away from the children, scrap half your music, edit your museums and your picture galleries; bowdlerize your Old Testament and rewrite your histories."

"You used to be a literary little cuss," he said at length; "didn't you edit the magazine before you left?"

Woollett has a Review—which Mrs. Newsome, for the most part, magnificently pays for and which I, not at all magnificently, edit.

Finding that one hand was not equal to the task, Edward offered his brother five dollars for each biography; he made the same offer to one or two journalists whom he knew and whose accuracy he could trust; and he was speedily convinced that merely to edit biographies written by others, at one-half the price paid to him, was more profitable than to write himself. Only by the simplest rules of psychology can he edit rightly so that he may lead, and to the average editor of to-day, it is to be feared, psychology is a closed book. The editor of *The New York Times* asked Bok to conduct for that newspaper a prize contest for the best American-designed dresses and hats, and edit a special supplement presenting them in full colors, the prizes to be awarded by a jury of six of the leading New York women best versed in matters of dress. For one man to edit two magazines inevitably meant a distribution of effort, and this Mr. Curtis counseled against. Doctor Anna Howard Shaw had been appointed chairman of the *National Committee of the Women's Council of National Defense*, and Bok arranged at once with her that she should edit a department page in his magazine, setting forth the plans of the committee and how the women of America could co-operate therewith.

It is a subject in which everybody is interested, and about which it is not polite to say that anybody is not well informed; for, although there are scattered through the land many persons, I am sorry to say, unable to pay for a newspaper, I have never yet heard of anybody unable to edit one.

What a dreary waste life in our office must have been before Miss Larrabee came to us to edit a society page for the paper!

He went to Europe again to prepare himself, and after entering upon his work as a teacher made a happy second marriage, served for four years as the first editor of *The Atlantic*, and helped his friend Charles Eliot Norton edit *The North American Review*. But Sparks proceeded to write another biography of Washington and to edit his writings.

That the propositions I have endeavored to establish have a direct bearing in various ways upon the qualifications of whoever undertakes to edit the works of Shakespeare will, I think, be apparent to those who consider the matter. That Shakespeare did not edit his own works must be attributed, we suspect, to his premature death.

During his thirteen years of travel (a more detailed account of which will be given in a subsequent chapter), he found time to revise and edit the books which appear to have formed the common stock-in-trade for all China; one of his ideas was to eliminate from these all sentiments of an anti-imperial nature.

It was the expressed intention of the Abbe Brasseur to edit the original text with his translation, but this he did not live to accomplish.

The object of this effort of Sir Henry Tyler's was obvious enough, and Mr. Bradlaugh commented: "The above letters make it pretty clear that Sir Henry W. Tyler having failed in his endeavor to get the science classes stopped at the Hall of Science, having also failed in his attempt to induce Sir W. Vernon Harcourt to prosecute myself and Mrs. Besant as editors and publishers of this journal, desires to make me personally and criminally responsible for the contents of a journal I neither edit nor publish, over which I have not a shadow of control, and in which I have not the smallest interest.

This paper will have, of course, many pages of business advertisements, and these will usually be well worth looking through, for the more intelligent editors of the days to come will edit this department just like any other, and classify their advertisements in a descending scale of freshness and interest that will also be an ascending scale of price.

I did edit the two first numbers.

Can I be a merchant, and the president of a bank, and a director in a life insurance company, and a school commissioner, and help edit a paper, and supervise the politics of our ward, and run for Congress?

You ought to edit a riddle book, Bertie, my son.

We'll buy a press, hire a printer, and Beth and Louise will help me edit the paper. But this is to be a newspaper reflecting the excitement of the entire world, Beth, and all the telegraphic news of a sporting character you must edit and arrange for our reading columns. "I—we—that is—we are three quite respectable young women who have under-taken to edit the *Millville Daily Tribune*, and the people we have secured to assist us are all—all quite desirable, in their way. So—; ahem! —so—" But she can't edit the telegraph news.

On the death of Mr. John Howard Clark, which took place at this time, Mr. John Harvey Finlayson was left to edit *The Register*, and I became a regular outside contributor to *The Register* and *The Observer*.

A little before the date of my resignation, Mr. James Virtue, the printer and publisher, had asked me to edit a new magazine for him, and had offered me a salary of £1000 a year for the work over and above what might be due to me for my own contributions.

Normans still edit his works—and dedicate these books to the town which also bred Corneille.

How to Write

845

Nahum took some blossoms to Arkham and showed them to the editor of the *Gazette*, but that dignitary did no more than write a humorous article about them, in which the dark fears of rustics were held up to polite ridicule. Ammi is such a good old man—when the reservoir gang gets to work I must write the chief engineer to keep a sharp watch on him. He would write of what he knew before death came, but his wife must not guess. This may be goodbye—if it is, write my son George Goodenough Akeley, 176 Pleasant St., San Diego, Cal., but don't come up here. Write the boy if you don't hear from me in a week, and watch the papers for news. Write my son George if you don't hear soon. Having sent home for most of his books, Blake bought some antique furniture suitable for his quarters and settled down to write and paint—living alone, and attending to the simple housework himself. There was much more than I could remember, but even what I did remember each morning would be enough to stamp me as a madman or a genius if ever I dared write it down. And all were urged to write copiously in their own languages of themselves and their respective periods; such documents to be filed in the great central archives. Of the animals I saw, I could write volumes. He meant to write you, but was delayed. Dr. Boyle will write later. I can scarcely bear to write it down in black and white even now, but perhaps that will not be necessary. Those investigations and discoveries have left their mark upon him; so that his voice trembles when he tells them, and his hand trembles when he tries to write of them. And againe I ask that you shalle write me as Jedediah and not Simon. Of his proposed itinerary he would say nothing save that the needs of his studies would carry him to many places, but he promised to write his parents fully and faithfully. Of his daily life he wrote by little, for there was little to write. The formula was so plainly audible in the hall outside the locked door that Mrs. Ward could not help memorizing it as she waited and listened anxiously, and later on she was able to write it down at Dr. Willett's request. *Sshh!*— write! Early in July Willett ordered Mrs. Ward to Atlantic City for an indefinite recuperative sojourn, and cautioned both Mr. Ward and the haggard and elusive Charles to write her only cheering letters. On the *source* of Slater's visions they speculated at length, for since he could neither read nor write, and had apparently never heard a legend or fairy-tale, his gorgeous imagery was quite inexplicable. His money and lands were gone, and he did not care for the ways of the people about him, but preferred to dream and write of his dreams. What he wrote was laughed at by those to whom he showed it, so that after a time he kept his writings to himself, and finally ceased to write. He was always nervous, though, about what some of the young fellows in Paris might write home to their relatives after the news of the marriage spread around. I had the agent write him that our affairs absolutely required one of us to go East, and of course my illness made it clear that I could not be the one. He it is that we have chosen to blend into one glorious whole all the beauty that the world hath known before, and to write words wherein shall echo all the wisdom and the loveliness of the past. One of them had wagered him a heavy sum that he could not—despite many poignant things to his credit in the *Dublin Review*—even write a truly interesting story of New York low life; and now, looking back, he perceived that cosmic irony had justified the prophet's words while secretly confuting their flippant meaning. Subsequently he seemed to be satisfied, and crossing to a chair by the table wrote a brief note, handed it to me, and returned to the table, where he began to write rapidly and incessantly. Then the glass broke shiveringly under the persistent impacts, and the chill wind rushed in, making the candles sputter and rustling the sheets of paper on the table where Zann had begun to write out his horrible secret. When first I saw that I must go, I prepared my diving suit, helmet, and air regenerator for instant donning, and immediately commenced to write this hurried chronicle in the hope that it may some day reach the world. This demoniac laughter which I hear as I write comes only from my own weakening brain. Tell me why that thing that calls itself Asenath writes differently off guard, so that you can't tell its script from—I'm too far gone to talk—I couldn't manage to telephone—but I can still write.

767

You need not be prompted to write with the appearance of sorrow for his disappointment. A woman is not to marry a man merely because she is asked, or because he is attached to her, and can write a tolerable letter. Emma felt the bad taste of her friend, but let it pass with a very true; and it would be a small consolation to her, for the clownish manner which might be offending her every hour of the day, to know that her husband could write a good letter. Why will not you write one yourself for us, Mr. Elton? It is one thing, said she, presently—her cheeks in a glow—to have very good sense in a common way, like every body else, and if there is anything to say, to sit down and write a letter, and say just what you must, in a short way; and another, to write verses and charades like this. Oh! Miss Woodhouse, what a pity that I must not write this beautiful charade into my book! Leave out the two last lines, and there is no reason why you should not write it into your book. Give me the book, I will write it down, and then there can be no possible reflection on you. We admired it so much, that I have ventured to write it into Miss Smith's collection. He may be sure of every woman's approbation while he writes with such gallantry. He can sit down and write a fine flourishing letter, full of professions and falsehoods, and persuade himself that he has hit upon the very best method in the world of preserving peace at home and preventing his father's having any right to complain. You who are such a judge, and write so beautifully yourself. That is what she writes about. Well, now I have just given you a hint of what Jane writes about, we will turn to her letter, and I am sure she tells her own story a great deal better than I can tell it for her. He had a great regard for Mrs. Goddard; and Emma should write a line, and invite her. Isabella and Emma, I think, do write very much alike. Isabella and Emma both write beautifully, said Mr. Woodhouse; and always did. Mr. Frank Churchill writes one of the best gentleman's hands I ever saw. Do not you remember, Mrs. Weston, employing him to write for you one day? Oh! when a gallant young man, like Mr. Frank Churchill, said Mr. Knightley dryly, writes to a fair lady like Miss Woodhouse, he will, of course, put forth his best. I shall write to Mrs. Partridge in a day or two, and shall give her a strict charge to be on the look-out for any thing eligible. So Frank writes word. Still Mrs. Elton insisted on being authorized to write an acquiescence by the morrow's post. It is not everybody that would have stood out in such a kind way as she did, and refuse to take Jane's answer; but she positively declared she would *not* write any such denial yesterday, as Jane wished her; she would wait—and, sure enough, yesterday evening it was all settled that Jane should go. Miss Fairfax was not well enough to write; He told me at parting, that he should soon write; and he spoke in a manner which seemed to promise me many particulars that could not be given now. Mrs. Weston had set off to pay the visit in a good deal of agitation herself; and in the first place had wished not to go at all at present, to be allowed merely to write to Miss Fairfax instead, and to defer this ceremonious call till a little time had passed, and Mr. Churchill could be reconciled to the engagement's becoming known; as, considering every thing, she thought such a visit could not be paid without leading to reports:—but Mr. Weston had thought differently; he was extremely anxious to shew his approbation to Miss Fairfax and her family, and did not conceive that any suspicion could be excited by it; or if it were, that it would be of any consequence; for such things, he observed, always got about. My courage rises while I write. What a letter the man writes! You see how delightfully she writes. But I am not afraid of your seeing what he writes. He writes like a sensible man. Who was so useful to him, who so ready to write his letters, who so glad to assist him?

648

I will write a letter to my wife and one to my daughter Kate. I will now step on board my ship and write some letters, which I shall ask you to take to Bridgetown with you. Go down to Captain Marchand's cabin an' write your letters. The captain of the pirates sat down in his well-furnished little room to write his letters, and the noise and confusion on deck, the swearing and the singing and the shouting to be heard everywhere, did not seem to disturb him in the least. Captain Marchand and Greenway had been waiting in anxious expectation for the return of Bonnet, and wondering how in the world a man could bring his mind to write letters at such a time as this. So he merely touched upon Major Bonnet and his vessel, and hoped that she might soon write to him and tell him what she cared for him to know, what she cared for him to tell to the people of Bridgetown, and what she wished to repose confidentially to his honour. It was perfectly plain, even to Dame Charter, that things had been said in Bridgetown which Mr. Newcombe had not cared to write. I had not thought of your seeing him, Dickory, and I did not write to him, but you will know what to say. He came to this vessel to bring me a message from my daughter, but he is an ill-bred stripling, and can neither read nor write. You write well and read, I know that, my good Sir Nightcap; and, moreover, you are a fair hand at figures. The only shrewd thing I ever knew your Sir Nightcap to do was to tell me you could not read nor write. Had it not been so I should have sent you to the town to help with the shore end of my affairs, and then you would have been there still and I should have had no admiral to write my log and straighten my accounts. He raised himself upon his elbow, he clutched at the paper, and clapping it upon the deck began to write. And this on a letter written in the dying moments of an English captain, a high and mighty captain who must have loved as few men love, to write that letter, his life's blood running over the paper as he wrote. At the very end of my life I write to you that you have escaped the fiercest love that ever a man had for a woman. Having finished these business details, Mr. Delaplaine went on and read aloud, and in the succeeding portion of the letter Mr. Newcombe begged Mr. Delaplaine to believe that it was the hardest duty of his whole life to write what he was now obliged to write, but that he knew he must do it, and therefore would not hesitate. Briefly and tersely, but with tears in the very ink, so sad were the words, the writer assured Mr. Delaplaine that his love for his niece had been, and was, the overpowering impulse of his life; that to win this love he had dared everything, he had hoped for everything, he had been willing to pass by and overlook everything, but that now, and it tore his heart to write it, his evil fortune had been too much for him; he could do anything for the sake of his love that a man with respect for himself could do, but there was one thing at which he must stop, at which he must bow his head and submit to his fate—he could not marry the daughter of an executed felon. When Mr. Robertson writes of the sea, the tang of the brine and the snap of the sea-breeze are felt behind his words. Mr. Bullen writes with a sympathy and pathetic touch rare indeed.

637

I thought—it seemed to me that perhaps I'm best qualified to write—Why you should write about the Middle Ages, I don't know. Tell me and I'll write it down. On the contrary, I'd feel that it being a meaningless world, why write? Why don't you write him up? Why don't you write a story about that place? I wish our Richard would write about her. But after you've all gone I'll be saying things for new Dicks to write down, and listening to the disillusions and cynicisms and emotions of new Anthonys—yes, and talking to new Glorias about the tans of summers yet to come. From his undergraduate days as editor of *The Harvard Crimson* Richard Caramel had desired to write. Any amiable young man, his head ringing with the latest crusade, could accomplish as much as he could with the débris of Europe—and it was time for him to write. He had followed it with the eyes of a journalist, for he was going to write a book about her some day. "I always say," said Muriel earnestly, "that if I ever had time to write down all my experiences it'd make a wonderful book." I'll write a play for you. "I'd like to take Gloria abroad," he complained, "except for this damn war—and next to that I'd sort of like to have a place in the country, somewhere near New York, of course, where I could write—or whatever I decide to do." Meanwhile you take a piece of paper and write down the names of seven possible towns. You mean write trash? But the really awful days aren't when I think I can't write. Well, why don't you go over and write about these Germans? Write something real, something about what's going on, something people can read. No wonder I can't write! Let's persuade our more erotic poets to write about the delights of the flesh, and induce some of our robust journalists to contribute stories of famous amours. I wish I could write. Early in the winter, when all conversation turned on the probability of America's going into the war, when Anthony was making a desperate and sincere attempt to write, Muriel Kane arrived in New York and came immediately to see them. There were six altogether, six wretched and pitiable efforts to "write down" by a man who had never before made a consistent effort to write at all. For a week they had corresponded passionately, almost hysterically—then by an unwritten agreement they had ceased to write more than twice, and then once, a week. She suddenly ceased to write about coming South. The darkness, alive with insects, beat in upon the mosquito-netting, beneath the shelter of which Anthony was trying to write a letter. To do this it had been necessary to write his broker for money. I've tried to write you again and again but it just seems to make things worse. She decided to write him word of her coming, but postponed the announcement upon the advice of Mr. Haight, who expected almost weekly that the case was coming up for trial. A "Heart Talk" is a little book in which I started, about five years ago, to write down what I had discovered were the principal reasons for a man's failure and the principal reasons for a man's success—from John D. Rockefeller back to John D. Napoleon (laughter), and before that, back in the days when Abel sold his birthright for a mess of pottage. Have you tried to write any—lately? I always thought that you and Maury would write some day, and now he's grown to be a sort of tight-fisted aristocrat, and you're—He himself had tried his best to write with his tongue in his cheek.

522

If you want to discuss what I say, please don't bother to write it down until later on, I don't have any time to waste and I'll soon be leaving. And he writes so many reports. You say these officials are lazy, but they're certainly not all lazy, especially this examining judge, he writes ever such a lot. Everyone had gone, but the examining judge, he stayed in the hall, I had to bring him a lamp in, all I had was a little kitchen lamp but he was very satisfied with it and started to write straight away. What I mean, with all this, I just wanted to tell you how the examining judge really does write lots of reports, especially about you as questioning you was definitely one of the main things on the agenda that Sunday. If he writes reports as long as that they must be of some importance. She writes; I have not seen Josef for a long time, I was in the bank last week but Josef was so busy that they would not let me through; I waited there for nearly an hour but then I had to go home as I had my piano lesson. Things like this don't come all of a sudden, they start developing a long time beforehand, there must have been warning signs of it, why didn't you write to me? However, when this happens, you should never trust them too far, as however firmly they may have declared this new point of view in favour of the defendant they might well go straight back to their offices and write a report for the court that says just the opposite, and might well be even harder on the defendant than the original view, the one they insist they've been fully dissuaded from. Earlier, just a week or so before, he could only have felt shame at the thought of being made to write out such documents himself; it had never entered his head that the task could also be difficult. I'll go there, he said as he took his leave of the manufacturer at the door, or, as I'm very busy at present, I'll write to him, perhaps he would like to come to me in my office some time. But despite seeming calm on the outside he was actually very shocked; he had told the manufacturer he would write to Titorelli only to show him in some way that he valued his recommendations and would consider the opportunity to speak with Titorelli without delay, but if he had thought Titorelli could offer any worthwhile assistance he would not have delayed. Now, at least, he found himself quite unable to understand how he could have intended to write to Titorelli and invite him into the bank. If that's what you want I'll write down an assertion of your innocence on a piece of paper. K. listened to all of this, testing it and thinking it over as if he had been given the task of closely observing everything spoken here, inform a higher office about it and write a report.

485

She inquired how long they had been dead: then how old I was, what was my name, whether I could read, write, and sew a little: then she touched my cheek gently with her forefinger, and saying, She hoped I should be a good child, dismissed me along with Miss Miller. I know something of Mr. Lloyd; I shall write to him; if his reply agrees with your statement, you shall be publicly cleared from every imputation; to me, Jane, you are clear now. Listen, then, Jane Eyre, to your sentence: to-morrow, place the glass before you, and draw in chalk your own picture, faithfully, without softening one defect; omit no harsh line, smooth away no displeasing irregularity; write under it, "Portrait of a Governess, disconnected, poor, and plain." It is my intention to write shortly and desire her to come to me at Madeira. Now act as you please: write and contradict my assertion—expose my falsehood as soon as you like. In that field, Adèle, I was walking late one evening about a fortnight since—the evening of the day you helped me to make hay in the orchard meadows; and, as I was tired with raking swaths, I sat down to rest me on a stile; and there I took out a little book and a pencil, and began to write about a misfortune that befell me long ago, and a wish I had for happy days to come: I was writing away very fast, though daylight was fading from the leaf, when something came up the path and stopped two yards off me. I will write to Madeira the moment I get home, and tell my uncle John I am going to be married, and to whom: if I had but a prospect of one day bringing Mr. Rochester an accession of fortune, I could better endure to be kept by him now. No, he said coolly: when you have indicated to us the residence of your friends, we can write to them, and you may be restored to home. But three of the number can read: none write or cipher. These could already read, write, and sew; and to them I taught the elements of grammar, geography, history, and the finer kinds of needlework. Write to Diana and Mary to-morrow, I said, and tell them to come home directly. What I want is, that you should write to your sisters and tell them of the fortune that has accrued to them. He cannot now see very distinctly: he cannot read or write much; but he can find his way without being led by the hand: the sky is no longer a blank to him—the earth no longer a void. I know that a stranger's hand will write to me next, to say that the good and faithful servant has been called at length into the joy of his Lord.

434

If you want to write good copy, you must be where the things are. Well, yes; I propose to write to him. Then for Heaven's sake, man, write it up! It was agreed that I should write home full accounts of my adventures in the shape of successive letters to McArdle, and that these should either be edited for the *Gazette* as they arrived, or held back to be published later, according to the wishes of Professor Challenger, since we could not yet know what conditions he might attach to those directions which should guide us to the unknown land. There it lies, even as I write, and there can be no question that it is the same. I will write again as the occasion serves. To-morrow (or to-day, rather, for it is already dawn as I write) we shall make our first venture into this strange land. When I shall be able to write again—or if I ever shall write again—I know not. I write this from day to day, but I trust that before I come to the end of it, I may be able to say that the light shines, at last, through our clouds. Some day, when I have a better desk than a meat-tin and more helpful tools than a worn stub of pencil and a last, tattered note-book, I will write some fuller account of the Accala Indians—of our life amongst them, and of the glimpses which we had of the strange conditions of wondrous Maple White Land. All this I shall some day write at fuller length, and amidst these more stirring days I would tenderly sketch in these lovely summer evenings, when with the deep blue sky above us we lay in good comradeship among the long grasses by the wood and marveled at the strange fowl that swept over us and the quaint new creatures which crept from their burrows to watch us, while above us the boughs of the bushes were heavy with luscious fruit, and below us strange and lovely flowers peeped at us from among the herbage; or those long moonlit nights when we lay out upon the shimmering surface of the great lake and watched with wonder and awe the huge circles rippling out from the sudden splash of some fantastic monster; or the greenish gleam, far down in the deep water, of some strange creature upon the confines of darkness. But already, as I write, a week has passed, and we have had our momentous interview with Lord John Roxton and—well, perhaps things might be worse.

271

Two other friends and myself agreed to write each a story founded on some supernatural occurrence. Continue for the present to write to me by every opportunity: I may receive your letters on some occasions when I need them most to support my spirits. I write a few lines in haste, to say that I am safe, and well advanced on my voyage. He composed heroic songs, and began to write many a tale of enchantment and knightly adventure. It was said; and we retired under the pretence of seeking repose, each fancying that the other was deceived: but when at morning's dawn I descended to the carriage which was to convey me away, they were all there—my father again to bless me, Clerval to press my hand once more, my Elizabeth to renew her entreaties that I would write often, and to bestow the last feminine attentions on her playmate and friend. You are forbidden to write—to hold a pen; yet one word from you, word will be a blessing to us. Adieu! my cousin; take care of yourself; and, I entreat you, write! I will write instantly, and relieve them from the anxiety they must feel. You have probably waited impatiently for a letter to fix the date of your return to us; and I was at first tempted to write only a few lines, merely mentioning the day on which I should expect you. He entreated me to write often. I write to you encompassed by peril and ignorant whether I am ever doomed to see again dear England, and the dearer friends that inhabit it.

200

At times I tell myself I dare not: that you will laugh, and cast me aside as a fabricator; and then again I pick up my pen and collect the scattered pages, for I *MUST* write it—the pallid splendour of that thing I loved, and won, and lost is ever before me, and will not be forgotten. I must and will write—it relieves me; read and believe as you list. Quicker than I can write it lapped a corner over and rolled me in its folds like a chrysalis in a cocoon. Over the lapping of the water in my ears I heard their sigh—like cries of admiration and surprise, the rattle of spray on the canoe sides mingled with the splash of oars, the flitting shadows of their prows were all about us, and in less time than it takes to write we were hauled aboard, revived, and taken to Hath's barge. It is not likely, if he has gone off on the razzle-dazzle, as I am sure he has, he is going to write every post and tell you about it. You shall write a book about that extraordinary story you told me just now.

194

If your ballpoint pen won't write as you want it to, your life doesn't stop, she probably was thinking. I write my letters with him too. He seemed to love to write more than to sketch. I don't see how he could stand up on end to write for very long, even with such a magnificent philosophy to bolster him. He won't write anything else! Proudly he continued to write his *Rise and Fall of the Western Plainsman* in a lucid, passionate prose which would evoke an imperishable picture—but in three thousand pages. From now on *he can write whatever he likes*! But most of his knowledge of Earth has come from books; he can't write classics about living things unless he sees living things. I feel, as a result, that I have observed this type of data to the extent that I can write of it competently without further study. It is fundamental that if you are to write serious literature, you must rub your nose against the realities of life. But if you aren't going to write serious literature, who will I get to go on my painting trips with me?

193

What is it his dear love has found in her fond heart to write Paul Lessingham? So!—That is what his dear love has found it in her heart to write Paul Lessingham!—Paul Lessingham! I warn you, Miss Lindon, that, until death, you will have to write me down your lover. If it is true that, now and again, Providence does write a man's character on his face, then there can't be the slightest shred of a doubt that a curious one's been written on his. I repeat that I write "my Marjorie" because, to me, she will always be "my" Marjorie! In some respects, he is a genius; in others—I will not write fool, for that he never is, though he has often done some extremely foolish things. Then, if this time I don't find out the how and the why and the wherefore of that charming conjuring trick, I'll give you leave to write me down an ass,—with a great, big A. I cannot utter the words the stranger uttered, I cannot even write them down. You write me down an ass! Write me down an ass again!

191

And because of this conviction I have determined to write down the story of the interesting periods of my life and of my death. That I have taken moments to write down a part of what occurred as that blow fell does not signify that I remained inactive for any such length of time. What it has taken minutes to write occurred in but a few seconds, but during that time Tars Tarkas had seen my plight and had dropped from the lower branches, which he had reached with such infinite labour, and as I flung the last of my immediate antagonists from me the great Thark leaped to my side, and again we fought, back to back, as we had done a hundred times before. Go then, through the burrows of the Ulsios, to The Gate of Enemies and carry to Floran the message that I shall write in his own language. Come, while I write the message. I will write them here at the close of my message to him, for the walls have ears, Ghek, while none but a Gatholian may read what I have written to Floran.

167

Louis writes; Susan writes; Neville writes; Jinny writes; even Bernard has now begun to write. But I cannot write. We shall write our exercises in ink here. We are all phrases in Bernard's story, things he writes down in his notebook under A or under B. I can write the letter straight off which I have begun ever so many times. I will write a quick, running, small hand, exaggerating the down stroke of the "y" and crossing the "t" thus—with a dash. No, I will write the letter tomorrow directly after breakfast. What did I write last night if it was not good poetry? Then he stretches his hand for his copy-book—a neat volume bound in mottled paper—and writes feverishly long lines of poetry, in the manner of whomever he admires most at the moment. When Louis is alone he sees with astonishing intensity, and will write some words that may outlast us all. This is poetry if we do not write it.

157

If you should write a fable for little fishes, you would make them speak like great whales. At the time I now write of, Father Mapple was in the hardy winter of a healthy old age; that sort of old age which seems merging into a second flowering youth, for among all the fissures of his wrinkles, there shone certain mild gleams of a newly developing bloom—the spring verdure peeping forth even beneath February's snow. I guess, Quohog there don't know how to write, does he? But were the coming narrative to reveal in any instance the complete abasement of poor Starbuck's fortitude, scarce might I have the heart to write it; for it is a thing most sorrowful, nay shocking, to expose the fall of valour in the soul. Nor smile so, while I write that this little black was brilliant, for even blackness has its brilliancy; behold yon lustrous ebony, panelled in king's cabinets.

139

Write soon. Don't write him—don't give him a chance to—well to suggest courteously that you'd better not come just yet. I'm sorry I did not write you more plainly. And when she rested she could not always converse, or read, or write. I'm surely glad for a good excuse to write you. Won't you write me? I'll never—never write him again. Yet shamed one moment at the consciousness she would write Glenn again and again, and exultant the next with the clamouring love, she seemed to have climbed beyond the self that had striven to forget. He didn't write it to me, but I know ... I'm wise. Will you write me how you are getting along? Carley knew she should sit down at her table and write and figure, but she could not do it then.

115

During an illness last winter I exhausted my store of those aids to cheerfulness, and was driven to write one for myself. No sooner was he over the threshold than he made a dash for my back room, where I used to smoke and write my letters. "I want to write books," he said. I want to see life, to travel the world, and write things like Kipling and Conrad. My first impulse had been to write a letter to the Prime Minister, but a little reflection convinced me that that would be useless. First, I want you to write a letter to your uncle. I'll write to the Permanent Secretary at the Foreign Office.

97

He picked up his pen half-heartedly, wondering whether he could find something more to write in the diary. Even when you write it you're still thinking in Oldspeak. I've read some of those pieces that you write in "The Times" occasionally. Where the Lottery was concerned, even people who could barely read and write seemed capable of intricate calculations and staggering feats of memory. It was important to write something down. But you write it very elegantly. Write it down and I'll sign it—anything! He began to write down the thoughts that came into his head.

85

Anyhow I've no starry calculations to be interfered with, and no immortal works to write. She was thrilled by her contact with a man of the upper class, this titled gentleman, this author who could write books and poems, and whose photograph appeared in the illustrated newspapers. And write to me if there is any news, and tell me about Sir Clifford, how he is. They had agreed not to write at all, but now she wanted to hear from him personally. Let him write!

82

Some jerk wants to write up a bunch of lousy report slips, make him look good, we're—Teacher ran him out for a late slip and he got me to write him up. He already had a write-up. I thought my write-up was pretty clear. How much did that youngster offer you to write up that incident the way you did? You will now write the words, "forgery, no genuine contract," over these pages. You will write as I told you—Now!

82

I hate to lose you for so long, and we shall not even be able to write. You'll have to write your sweet nothings, instead of saying Them. You should write a book and put some of those things in it. Bode's law, you know, says, Write down 0, 3, 6, 12, 24, 48, 96. Oh, that I had now their opportunities, that I might write a thesis that should live forever, and save millions of souls from the anguish of mine!

63

Why was that corner chosen to write it on? When a man writes on a wall, his instinct leads him to write about the level of his own eyes. Above all, why should the second man write up the German word *RACHE* before decamping? I don't know what it was that put it into my head to write upon the wall with it.

60

I rested from work for some days after this, and was in a mind to write an account of the whole affair to wake up English physiology. There is much that sticks in my memory that I could write,—things that I would cheerfully give my right hand to forget; but they do not help the telling of the story.

55

The captain, as a practical man equal to all difficulties, began to write with frightful rapidity. "Beg pardon, lieutenant but cannot President Barbicane write?" Very well; let our industrious friends construct a giant alphabet; let them write words three fathoms long, and sentences three miles long, and then they can send us news of themselves.

52

Like all men of the Library, I have traveled in my youth; I have wandered in search of a book, perhaps the catalogue of catalogues; now that my eyes can hardly decipher what I write, I am preparing to die just a few leagues from the hexagon in which I was born.

44

You are well aware that chemical preparations exist, and have existed time out of mind, by means of which it is possible to write upon either paper or vellum, so that the characters shall become visible only when subjected to the action of fire.

42

But yes, I can also write poetry. And write? It is very good that you're able to read and write, very good. And would you write something for me on this piece of paper? It is excellent how you're able to write.

41

Think too for whom you write, I pray! I write, "In the beginning was the Deed!" Shall I with chisel, pen, or graver write? Yet write away without cessation, as at the Holy Ghost's dictation! He writes and returns the book.

34

They are expressed in the most plain and simple terms, wherein those people are not mercurial enough to discover above one interpretation; and to write a comment upon any law is a capital crime.

32

When one writes a novel about grown people, he knows exactly where to stop—that is, with a marriage; but when he writes of juveniles, he must stop where he best can.

28

That is exactly what the dreamer can do, and no one else but he; and Mr. Stephen is himself a dreamer when he writes and feels like this.

28

It recedes with the years, and I write out my life longhand, a letter to the me that I'll be when it's restored into a clone somewhere, somewhen.

23

Owing to their historical position, it became the vocation of the aristocracies of France and England to write pamphlets against modern bourgeois society.

22

It is disagreeable for me to recall and write these things, but I set them down that my story may lack nothing.

22

Yes, but if you shout in my ear like that again, you'll have to write things out for me for ever after.

21
Nevertheless that pencil must scrawl broadly over the sky, and for a long time, merely hoping to write on its target.

12
Perhaps you can write to me. You will write, at any rate.

12
Have you been *reading* the stuff you write? I can't write it.

8
"I did not write that message," he stated.

5
Never mind, I'll write it.

NOTES

NOTHING ODD CAN LAST consists of 36 alphabetized questions from *Coles Notes*-style websites on Laurence Sterne's *The Life and Opinions of Tristram Shandy, Gentleman.*

AND THEN THERE WERE NONE is a record of every number or amount word in Agatha Christie's novel of the same title.

THE EDITOR: A DETECTIVE STORY is an exhaustive record of every sentence that contains the word "editor" (lifted unaltered and in published order) in *The Bat* (1920) by Mary Roberts Rinehart and Avery Hopwood. The original text formed the inspiration for Bob Kane's creation of Batman.

WILD ROSE COUNTRY is every piece of text within one block of my home.

CROSS IT OVER IT is a series of pornographic instructions pertaining both to tying a tie and to composing poetry.

I CAN SEE THE WHOLE ROOM ... AND THERE'S NOBODY IN IT! is a re-contextualization of all the text in Roy Lichtenstein's oeuvre, 1963–1973.

I stole IF YOU HAVE IT and A CHAIN SAW from an aftershave commercial and a spam email, respectively.

HOW TO EDIT: A is an exhaustive record of every incidence of the word "edit" in the over 1,100 different English-language texts stored at Project Gutenberg (www.gutenberg.org) which are indexed as starting with the letter *A*.

Sources:

Brinton, Daniel Garrison. *Aboriginal American Authors.* | Cicero, Marcus Tullius. (James Reid, ed.) *Academica.* | Strachey, John St. Loe. *The Adventure of Living: A Subjective Autobiography.* | Davis, Richard Harding. *Adventures and Letters of Richard Harding Davis.* | Quiller-Couch, Arthur Thomas. *Adventures in Criticism.* | Elwes, Alfred. *The Adventures of a Dog, and a Good Dog Too.* | Bulfinch, Thomas. *The Age of Chivalry.* | Allen, Percy Stafford. *The Age of Erasmus: Lectures Delivered in the Universities of Oxford and London.* | Lang, Andrew. *Alfred Tennyson.* | Jerome, Jerome K. *All Roads Lead to Calvary.* | Hornung, Ernest William. *The Amateur Cracksman.* | James, Henry. *The Ambassadors.* | Bok, Edward William. *The Americanization of Edward Bok: The Autobiography of a Dutch Boy Fifty Years After.* | Warner, Charles Dudley. *American Newspaper.* | Heydrick, Benjamin A., ed. *Americans All: Stories of American Life of To-Day.* | Perry, Bliss. *The American Spirit in Literature: A Chronicle of Great Interpreters.* | Lowell, James Russell. *Among My Books (First Series).* | Parker, Edward Harper. *Ancient China Simplified.* | Brinton, Daniel Garrison. *The Annals of the Cakchiquels.* | Besant, Annie Wood. *Annie Besant: An Autobiography.* | Wells, H.G. *Anticipations of the Reaction of Mechanical and Scientific Progress upon Human Life and Thought.* | Newman, John Henry. *Apologia pro Vita Sua.* | Talmage, T. De Witt. *Around The Tea-Table.* | Garvice, Charles. *At Love's Cost.* | Baum, L. Frank. *Aunt Jane's Nieces on Vacation.* |

Spence, Catherine Helen. *An Autobiography.* | Trollope, Anthony. *Autobiography of Anthony Trollope.* | Belloc, Hilaire. *Avril Being Essays on the Poetry of the French Renaissance.*

How to Write is an exhaustive record of every incidence of the words "write" or "writes" in 40 different English-language texts. These texts were picked aesthetically and to represent a disparate number of genres.

Sources:

Lovecraft, H.P. *Collected Stories.* | Austen, Jane. *Emma.* | Stockton, Frank R. *Kate Bonnet: The Romance of a Pirate's Daughter.* | Fitzgerald, F. Scott. *The Beautiful and Damned.* | Kafka, Franz. *The Trial.* | Brontë, Charlotte. *Jane Eyre: An Autobiography.* | cummings, e.e. *The Enormous Room.* | Doyle, Arthur Conan. *The Lost World.* | Shelley, Mary. *Frankenstein.* | Arnold, Edwin Lester Linden. *Gulliver of Mars.* | Marsh, Richard. *The Beetle.* | Banta, Frank. *Droozle.* | Burroughs, Edgar Rice. "The Barsoom series." | Woolf, Virginia. *The Waves.* | Melville, Herman. *Moby Dick.* | Grey, Zane. *The Call of the Canyon.* | Lawrence, D.H. *Lady Chatterley's Lover.* | Orwell, George. *Nineteen eighty-four.* | Buchan, John. *The Thirty-nine Steps.* | Astor, John Jacob. *A Journey in Other Worlds: A Romance of the Future.* | Doyle, Arthur Conan. *A Study in Scarlet.* | Wells, H.G. *The Island of Doctor Moreau.* | Verne, Jules. *From the Earth to the Moon.* | Borges, Jorge Luis. "The Library in Babel." | Cole, Everett B. *The Best Made Plans.* | Poe, Edgar Allan. "The Gold Bug." | Hesse, Hermann. *Siddhartha.* | von Goethe, Johann Wolfgang. *Faust Part 1.* | Swift, Jonathan. *Gulliver's Travels.* | Twain, Mark. *The Adventures of Tom Sawyer.* | Mallock, W.H. *Is Life Worth Living?* | Doctorow, Cory. *Down and Out in the Magic Kingdom.* | Marx, Karl, and Friedrich Engels. *The Communist Manifesto.* | Wells, H.G. *The War of the Worlds.* | Campbell, John W. *Invaders from the Infinite.* |

Anderson, Paul William. *The Burning Bridge.* | Eliot, T.S. *Prufrock and Other Observations.* | Collins, Les. *Question of Comfort.* | Robeson, Kenneth. *The Black Spot.* | Clifton, Mark Irvin. *Sense from Thought Divide.*

ACKNOWLEDGEMENTS

Thanks and gratitude to my friends and colleagues Jonathan Ball, Christian Bök, Craig Dworkin, Chris Ewart, Rob Fitterman, Kenneth Goldsmith, Helen Hajnoczky, Bill Kennedy, Robert Majzels, kevin mcpherson eckhoff, Simon Morris, Vanessa Place, Sina Queyras, Jordan Scott, the staff at Pages Books on Kensington, Nick Thurston and Darren Wershler.

Thank you also to my family and to Kristen.

How to Write and How to Edit: A were published through Kenneth Goldsmith's *Publishing the Unpublishable* series at ubuweb.com. Excerpts from How to Write also appeared in *NōD* magazine. How to Edit: A was commissioned by *OEI* and later appeared as chapbooks from No Press and above/ground. If You Have It and Nothing Odd Can Last originally appeared in *NōD* magazine. A Chain Saw originally appeared in *NōD* and *The White Wall Review.* The Editor originally appeared in *NōD* magazine and was also published in a graphic-fiction collaboration with Mark Laliberte (No Press, 2008). Wild Rose Country originally appeared as a broadsheet through above/ground press. I Don't Read was originally published as a leaflet by No Press.